POLAR
BEARS

Nikita Ovsyanikov

**WORLDLIFE
LIBRARY**

Voyageur Press

Contents

This adult male is probably more than ten years old. The scars on his face are reminders of his battles with other males in competition for females during courtship time. Some of the scars may also have resulted from hitting sharp ice edges while hunting.

Introduction

Every year by late August, when the first snows cover the muddy, uninhabited beaches of Wrangel Island's north coast, polar bear tracks appear on the shore. This is the time for the bears to visit the land of their birth. By the beginning of September, only a few bears will have set foot on this High Arctic island, but in a couple more weeks, the single lines of tracks will have grown into well-beaten trails made by the broadly spaced soles of dozens of polar bear feet.

Wrangel Island is the High Arctic frontier of eastern Siberia, lying in the Chukchi Sea at 71° N latitude and along the 180th meridian. Exposed to the north winds, this land is the first to face the cold breath of the coming Arctic winter. From early September on, it becomes a domain of fogs, snowstorms, piercing chill, and wet blizzards. The low, dense cloud cover rarely breaks to allow the sun, resting ever lower in the late-autumn sky, to add color to the grayish-white landscape.

Despite the weather, autumn is the most comfortable time of year for polar bears to visit Wrangel. Food is plentiful in the sea, and the pack ice floating around the island provides a solid platform from which to hunt. The heat of the summer is past, and the bears are curious to investigate a shore they have not seen for three or four months. The bears remain on the island only if the sea ice retreats and strands them there, or if they find a tremendous amount of food on shore, such as a walrus rookery or a beached whale. By the beginning of winter, the coast is deserted again. Only the pregnant females remain. Their smaller tracks—easily distinguished from those of the males—lead directly from the beach to the mountains, where they search for a place to build their maternity dens in the snow. They are here to give birth to a new generation of the largest non-aquatic predator in the world.

It was early November 1993 when my field assistant, Leonid Bove, and I were driving two snowmobiles along the north coast of Wrangel Island for our routine survey of polar bear distribution when I spotted some dark objects on the flat, land-fast ice. Through my binoculars I made out some twenty polar bears concentrated around a patch of rough ice on a frozen lagoon. Then I saw there were yellow bodies in all directions, some lying or rolling in the snow, others walking around. During the next twenty minutes Leonid and I counted exactly ninety-nine bears.

While Leonid looked after the snowmobiles, I climbed to the top of a ridge about two hundred yards from the main concentration of bears to get a better view. Bears of all ages, including mothers with cubs, were milling around a hole in the ice. Some were wet; others were stained yellowish brown as though they had been eating the remains of a large animal. About 165 feet (50 m) away from the hole, thirteen huge adult males were resting in shallow pits that had been excavated in the snow.

Two adult males enjoy a play fight. When polar bears are in good shape and not too busy with such vital activities as hunting or courtship, they are extremely playful animals.

The next day we returned. Whatever food had attracted the bears to the hole, it seemed the time of easy pickings was over. Some bears were still waiting to feed, while others were moving off onto the sea ice. At the end of the day, we drove our snowmobiles right up to the hole, scaring away all the bears except two adult males. One of them was sitting in the hole chewing on a large piece of gray skin; the other was circling as the hole was too narrow for the two bears to dive in simultaneously. The bears were so preoccupied that they paid no attention to us even when we pulled up 33 feet (10 m) away. We could now confirm what we had suspected: They were feeding on the remains of a whale. Gradually the other bears became accustomed to the noise of our engines and returned. Surrounded by polar bears anxious to scavenge what remained of the carcass, we sensed their excitement and, for a short while at least, felt that we were a part of their community.

Large congregations of polar bears around bountiful sources of food are not unusual events, yet when we think of polar bears we think of solitary hunters living out their lives in isolation on vast, empty expanses of ice. There is so much we have yet to learn about this bear of ice and snow. One reason we know so little about polar bears is that they live in a harsh environment far from human habitation. They spend most of their lives wandering great distances over drifting ice, where even the most technologically advanced means of transportation cannot follow them. There are only two seasons in the year when some polar

In autumn, before the ocean freezes, pack ice in the Arctic starts to push southward, and many polar bears come ashore on islands or the Arctic mainland to scout along the coasts.

bears appear on the shore: spring (during March and April) and autumn (from September through October).

Many generations of researchers working in difficult conditions have contributed to our present knowledge of polar bears. The first scientific descriptions of the polar bear were made in 1774 by British naval officer Constantine Phipps and in 1776 by Peter Pallas, head of the exploration division of the Academy of Sciences in St. Petersburg, Russia. We also have accounts from the pioneering expeditions of four centuries of Arctic explorers. Although these reports were often influenced by the observers' fear of unknown, hostile environments and large predators, they laid the foundation for further objective research.

To protect her two-year-old cub, a female bear lunges aggressively at an adult male who approached too close to her family. In social interactions within polar bear congregations, females with cubs display the most aggressive manners, although they are always protective.

In the 1920s and 1930s, technological progress opened a new era of intensive Arctic exploration. Many records of polar bear activity were made from polar research stations and from numerous expeditions surveying Arctic islands. This was a period of intensive fieldwork. Scientists surveyed polar bear habitats, looking for bear tracks and observing animals on foot, from low-flying airplanes, or from ships. The rapid expansion of human activity in the Arctic resulted in the accumulation of a significant amount of data on polar bear ecology and distribution. It also resulted in an unprecedented increase in human impact on the bears, mostly through direct persecution and shooting. Wherever human settlements appeared within traditional polar bear ranges, the bears were pushed away to more remote areas.

Today, polar bear conservation is a global priority, and research projects are being carried out by the five countries that include portions of the polar bear's circumpolar range: Russia, Norway, Greenland (Denmark), Canada, and Alaska (United States). Ground observations are still important, but other techniques have been developed that allow scientists to pose questions that could never have been answered by fieldwork alone.

Dozens of polar bears have been fitted with collars that emit radio signals. With the latest generation of batteries, movements of collared bears can be tracked via satellite for up to two years, helping scientists delineate the ranges of different polar bear populations. Although a few males have been collared, usually the collars are put on females because males, whose thick necks are as wide as their heads, easily lose the expensive transmitters. Molecular genetics is being used to determine the relationship of polar bears to other species of bear, and to help determine the borders of polar bear populations. DNA sequencing of blood and tissue samples is being used not only in scientific research but also in monitoring the take of bears by native populations. Chemical analysis of tissue is being used to record the level of toxic substances accumulated in the bodies of polar bears. The data gathered by scientists confirms how fragile the existence of this great bear is, even though it lives its life in such remote areas.

Whatever we humans are doing on Earth, polar bears live their lives oblivious to our accomplishments. Leaving the bears at the whale carcass, we head east to Cape Warring, where the mother bears are arriving at their traditional denning area. The bears are here to live; we are here to walk in their tracks to try to learn about their lives in this High Arctic environment. Wrangel Island is a strictly protected natural area, and nature here remains as it has been for centuries. Following polar bear trails in this remote wilderness, it is clear to us that it will be up to us humans to ensure that the next generations of polar bears do not lose their homelands.

The Ice Bear

Of the eight species of bears inhabiting our planet, the polar bear is the youngest and the largest. Four of these eight species are southern bears that inhabit subtropical forests: the sun bear, the sloth bear, the spectacled bear, and the giant panda. The four species of northern bears are the American and Asian black bears, the brown bear, and the polar bear.

Northern bears live in temperate forests (the two species of black bears and the brown bear) and the Arctic (the brown and polar bears). They are larger than their southern counterparts, with a more pronounced size difference between the sexes. Whereas southern bears are vegetarians who specialize in feeding on particular plants—the giant panda, for instance, subsists mainly on bamboo, which is available year round—northern bears are opportunistic feeders because they have to contend with seasonal changes in their food supply. Another adaptation to seasonal change is their ability to hibernate in the winter.

The polar bear is at the far end of this adaptive scale as the only bear that came to occupy an extreme ecological niche around the top of the world. Its Latin name, *Ursus maritimus,* means "marine bear," and no other terrestrial mammal, except for the Arctic fox, can penetrate as far into the Arctic Ocean.

The evolutionary history of bears can be traced by fossil remains to the early Miocene epoch, about twenty million years ago, when small and stocky bearlike predators—more like dogs than bears—appeared. The first representative of the family, the dawn bear, was about the size of a fox terrier and inhabited subtropical Europe for fifteen million years. Bears began to increase in size and number of species in the middle Pliocene, about five million years ago. This was when the first representative of the genus Ursus appeared. Ursus is the genus of all modern northern bears. At this time, the world's climate became drier, and steppes and savannas became the Northern Hemisphere's predominant landscapes. The high productivity and diversity of plant species in these expanding grasslands caused a rapid increase in the number and variety of both mammalian prey and predator species, a trend that continued through

A mother with two cubs-of-the-year passes across a frozen lagoon. During their first year, polar bear cubs stay close to their mother, especially when the family is on the move.

the late Pliocene and on into the Pleistocene epoch.

Scientists believe that the polar bear evolved in Siberia from an ancestral brown bear when a segment of the population became isolated by gradually advancing glaciers 250,000 to 200,000 years ago. The stranded bears were forced to forage in the sea and had to develop new behavioral, physiological, and

morphological features to survive changing and increasingly severe environmental conditions. Luckily, their previous evolutionary history had prepared them for such changes, as brown bears were already well adapted for life in the Temperate Zone with its pronounced seasonal changes and often-severe climate.

The actual evolution of polar bears is difficult to trace because of the scarcity of fossil remains. The ancestors of the polar bear lived and died out on the ice and in coastal areas, and the forces of nature rarely preserved their remains. The first polar bear fossils—fossil elbow bones from bears that died about 80,000 years ago—were discovered on the Yamal Peninsula in western Siberia in 1953 and in London in 1964. Subsequent discoveries uncovered younger remains in late Pleistocene deposits dated from 100,000 to 10,000 years ago in Scandinavia, Denmark, Germany, and northeastern Siberia. All available evidence suggests that the polar bear became a distinct species in the middle Pleistocene, approximately 250,000 to 100,000 years ago.

During late summer and autumn when the sea ice is broken into separate floes, females with small cubs prefer to stay on more substantial ground. Many of them come to Arctic islands, such as this mother with two cubs-of-the-year scouting along the coast of Wrangel Island in the Siberian Arctic.

Although polar and brown bears differ in appearance, genetically they are so similar that they have interbred in captivity to produce fertile offspring. What makes polar bears so different from brown bears are adaptations for their more predatory way of life in harsh marine-ice habitats. For example, polar bear claws are shorter, sharper, and more curved, characteristics better suited for rasping hard ice and capturing slippery prey than for digging plant roots or insects out of soft soil; polar bear molars have sharper cutting surfaces to tear flesh better. As the polar bear evolved, it developed a more elongate and streamlined body

A young male polar bear examines the edge of the sea ice where his usual prey—seals—can be found.

Healthy polar bears love to play fight with each other. Not only cubs and subadult bears, but adults, such as these two males, become playmates with astonishing enthusiasm.

shape with a relatively smaller head and longer neck. Polar bears are good swimmers and are able to swim 60 to 70 miles (100–120 km), and maybe even farther, without landing. Their webbed paws propel them through the water at speeds of up to 4 miles per hour (6.5 km/h). While diving, polar bears can remain underwater for up to two minutes. Polar bear ears are small and furry, and the soles of their paws are densely covered with hair so that only their toe pads and sole calluses are naked—significantly less exposed surface area than on the paws of brown bears.

Because the polar bears' environment is mainly white all year round, they too are white. Actually they are not pure white, but light yellow or cream colored depending on their location, activity, and the light conditions. Polar bears look almost pure white after living on clean ice and swimming in the sea. After they have been on shore for a while, their fur usually becomes yellowish brown as it picks up colors from the tundra and the beach.

A female polar bear leads her two cubs-of-the-year across hummocks wrapped in snow mist in the midst of a blizzard. Following their mother for two and half years, young bears will learn skills to survive in the harsh Arctic environment.

When polar bears eat fresh meat, their fur becomes stained with blood and blubber. The yellow color of their coat is thought to result from the oxidation of seal blubber, but this may not be the only reason. Female polar bears are yellow when they emerge from maternity dens. They have lain with their cubs for three months in the confined area of the den, and their fur is probably stained by the cubs' excretions. Polar bears that stay on shore for extended periods and feed on carrion may become almost as dark brown as their terrestrial relatives. Polar bears do like to clean themselves, however, and when their fur is stained with blood, blubber, or soil, they often crawl and roll in the snow, or splash around in the surf to wash.

Whatever color polar bear fur appears, the individual hairs are actually colorless and hollow, one of several adaptations for better protection against the cold. The hollow hairs are thought to function like optical fibers, transporting ultraviolet radiation to the bear's black skin, which stores the heat. Polar bear fur is denser than that of brown bears and is made up of two types of hair: guard hairs up to 6 inches (15 cm)

Dense fur along with a thick layer of underskin fat protects polar bears from the extremes of the Arctic climate. Long sleeping periods help to save energy and overcome particularly harsh days.

long extend over the dense, 2-inch (5-cm) hairs that make up the waterproof undercoat. The longest hairs on a polar bear, from 6 to 10 inches (16–26 cm), are on the inner surface of its forelegs.

Insulation from the cold is provided by both fur and fat. A thick layer of fat under the skin covers nearly all of the bear's body, including its head and the undersides of its paws. On the bear's rump, this layer of fat may be up to 5 inches (12 cm) thick. Polar bears also have layers of fat up to 1.6 inches (4 cm) thick between their muscles, and particularly plump individuals may even have fat deposits up to 1.2 inches (3 cm) thick around their internal organs. Remarkably, even after living exclusively on her fat deposits during four months of hibernation, a female can still have a 2-inch (5-cm) layer of fat on her back, 4 inches (10 cm) on her rump, and 1.2 to 2 inches (3–5 cm) on the soles of her paws. The total weight of the fat on an adult polar bear may exceed 220 pounds (100 kg), or 40 percent of the animal's total weight.

The weight of polar bears varies dramatically depending on where they live and the time of year. In the Canadian High Arctic, polar bears are larger than in the Norwegian archipelago of Svalbard and in eastern Greenland. In the Russian Arctic, there are two general groups of polar bears: the European or western bears and the Siberian or eastern bears. Siberian polar bears, including the bears in the Chukchi Sea region, are among the largest in the world. Mature Siberian polar bears can weigh from 1,760 to 2,200 pounds (800–1,000 kg), whereas over the rest of the Arctic the range is from 660 to 1,760 pounds (300–800 kg). The maximum known weight for a polar bear—2,204 pounds (1,002 kg)—was reported for a male killed in Alaska.

Females are normally about 50 to 75 percent of the males' weight, with a range of 330 to 880 pounds (150–400 kg) depending on the season and geographic region. The weight of females emerging from dens in the spring on Wrangel Island is from 392 to 660 pounds (178–300 kg). These weights are high not only because polar bears in the Chukchi Sea are bigger than polar bears in other regions of the Arctic, but also because hunting conditions around Wrangel are very favorable, and many females enter dens in the autumn in particularly good shape: after a good summer, they may weigh as much as 770 to 880 pounds (350–400 kg).

The size of polar bears is no less impressive than their weight. Adult males can measure up to 10 feet (300 cm), excluding the tail, but generally are from 6.5 to 8 feet (200–250 cm) long. Female body length without the tail is 5 to 8 feet (160–250 cm). The tail of a polar bear, including the hair, measures 8 to 8.8 inches (20–22 cm). Height at the shoulders for a bear standing on all fours is 4 to 4.5 feet (130–140 cm), rarely as tall as 5 feet (150 cm). The body length of newborn cubs is 12 inches (30 cm) for males and 11 inches (28 cm) for females.

Polar bears are not only the largest, they are also among the strongest terrestrial predators. They have exceptionally massive and powerful muscles, particularly in the neck, shoulders, and forelegs. Polar bear adaptations for living in a treacherous environment composed of massive blocks and solid sheets of crushing pack ice have been finely tuned over thousands of years. Keeping warm and surviving on fat deposits when food is scarce are two of these adaptations. Other adaptations depend on their enormous strength. For example, polar bears travel vast distances between and upon ice floes. They can easily jump over 6.5-foot (2-m) ice pressure ridges or down from sheer walls of ice that are 20 feet (6 m) high. Their power allows them to catch beluga whales weighing up to 1,320 pounds (600 kg) in narrow channels of open water and pull them out onto the ice. On Wrangel, I once tracked a bear that had dragged the 660-pound (300-kg) carcass of a young walrus 495 feet (150 m) across a gravel spit, then 990 feet (300 m) through the ice and slush of a lagoon, and finally 165 feet (50 m) up a 20-degree tundra slope. Small wonder that polar bears are well able to survive on their drifting continent of ice.

Adult walruses are difficult prey for polar bears. Facing off against an attacking polar bear male with her tusks, this female walrus stopped a male bear from trying to catch a calf.

The Super Predator

A cold wind is blowing streams of snow over the frozen Arctic Ocean. Tiny powdery crystals sparkle in the sun and fill the air, obscuring the icy landscape and the yellowish figure of a lone polar bear slowly making its way between the ice hummocks. No other living creature can be seen for miles in this chaotic jumble of pressure ridges, flat ice fields, and the occasional dark strips of open water that cut across the endless white expanse.

The bear, a fat adult male, apparently knows where he is headed in this white chaos. He must, or he would not have grown so big and beautiful. He walks from one hummock to another along the leeward sides of pressure ridges or follows the strips of open water. Confidently directed by lessons learned in his youth, he is surveying the places where his prey—seals—are likely to be found. Approaching one ice hummock, the bear stops with all his attention directed at the snow some 200 feet (60 m) ahead of him. Listening to the sounds coming from below, he moves slowly forward, methodically extending each fore-paw to touch and test the snow before gently pressing down on the sole as he takes another step. He knows exactly what he is doing: crunching snow could alert a seal to approaching danger.

A few more careful steps and the bear stops, remaining completely still. He stays motionless for about a minute, all his senses concentrated on the invisible object under the snow—head up, ears raised and turned forward, nose smelling the air. Then he springs into the air and charges forward in a series of long leaps before plowing into the snow and piercing the crust with one powerful strike of his forepaws. Almost at the same instant, he pushes his muzzle into the hole, bites a seal, and begins the struggle to pull it out onto the ice. The seal fights to escape, but the bear is stronger. In a few seconds the hunt is over. The bear drags his kill several yards away and opens the carcass. He will spend the next twelve hours alter-nately eating and sleeping, until he gorges himself.

Polar bears accumulate fat more efficiently when they eat fat than when they eat meat because they can digest fat more completely than they can digest protein. If prey is scarce, a polar bear consumes the whole carcass of a freshly killed seal; however, when seals are plentiful and hunting provides a surfeit of food, the bear eats only the fat off its prey, leaving the rest for scavengers. The first scavengers to arrive are other polar bears, particularly the young and females with cubs. Then Arctic foxes, ravens, and gulls take their turns at the carcass. These opportunists emerge from nowhere in this frozen desert as soon as a new bear kill appears. As a predator at the top of the food chain, the polar bear provides the means for many other species to survive on the ice.

The lifeless image applied to the Arctic pack ice is just as misleading as the lifeless image applied to the hotter, drier types of desert. Even in the middle of winter, life is not absent from the High Arctic; it is just hidden beneath the ice and snow to avoid the barrage of cutting winds and bitter cold. Both the lower surface of the ice and the sea bottom shelter many life forms, and these are especially plentiful along the edges of the pack ice. Here sunlight penetrates the surface, providing the energy aquatic plants need to photosynthesize.

Phytoplankton form the base of food chains in High Arctic ecosystems. These minute, free-floating aquatic plants provide nourishment for small animals called zooplankton, the first-level or primary consumers of organic material. Zooplankton, in turn, provide food for fish, the second-level consumers. Next in this food chain are the seals. Feeding on fish or shellfish, seals are second- or third-level consumers. Everywhere in the Arctic, polar bears hunt seals. Because the seal is itself a predator and a third-level consumer, this makes the polar bear a fourth-level consumer. There is no other non-aquatic mammalian predator anywhere in the world as high in the food chain as the polar bear. It is higher even than the archetypal predator, the wolf. For the wolf preys mainly on ungulates and rodents—primary consumers of organic material—which makes the wolf a second-level consumer. The only other mammal on Earth with an equivalent position within an ecosystem is the killer whale, *Orcinus orca,* an aquatic predator that feeds on fish, seals, sea lions, and walruses.

All predators depend on abundant, well-distributed, and consistently available prey in order to live and reproduce. The specific food resources that allowed the ancestors of polar bears to colonize Arctic sea-ice habitats were the two most common species of Arctic seal: the ringed seal, *Phoca hispida,* and the bearded seal, *Erignathus barbatus.* Both are plentiful in number and circumpolar in distribution.

The ringed seal is a small prey for the polar bear. Adults weigh from 66 to 176 pounds (30–80 kg) and measure about 3 to 4 feet (100–125 cm) in length. As a food supply, the ringed seal's small size is more than compensated for by its abundance and year-round availability. Ringed seals for polar bears in Arctic marine ecosystems are like lemmings for Arctic foxes in terrestrial ones: extremely important, but it takes a lot of them to make a meal.

Ringed seals are found throughout the entire Arctic Ocean, including mainland coastal waters, as well as in waters surrounding archipelagos in both the Western and Eastern Hemispheres. They roam widely and have been recorded right at the North Pole. The southern edge of the species' range extends to Newfoundland, Iceland, Jan Mayen Island, Bear Island, and the northern coasts and river estuaries of eastern Europe, Asia, and North America, including the Bering, Okhotsk, and White Seas. Ringed seals feed on fish and crustaceans. Although they are not restricted to shallow waters, the highest population densities are found at the edge of continental shelves. The world population is estimated at five million.

Female ringed seals prefer to give birth on stable, land-fast ice. Where snow conditions allow, they construct birthing dens beneath the snow in which to hide their pups. Usually, the birthing dens are distributed over a large area among the dens of adult seals. Dens are used by adults as resting spots when they haul out on the ice. They are constructed over breathing holes in deep snow around ice hummocks and along pressure ridges. In winter and early spring, when the ocean's surface is one solid sheet of ice, seals maintain a number of additional breathing holes close to these dens. One seal normally uses several breathing holes, and it is remarkable that even in the complete darkness of the polar night they can locate these holes in the constantly shifting sea of ice.

The Arctic pack ice provides good shelter against predators, and polar bears had to become not only powerful, but also very skillful hunters to successfully exploit this habitat. Sea ice is constantly changing; it is almost impossible to predict the shape or condition of the ice itself, let alone the activities below it. Separated from their prey by a thick sheet of ice, polar bears had to develop a number of different hunting strategies.

Seal pups in their birthing dens are the easiest prey. Even Arctic foxes actively search for and dig pups out of their birthing dens, and in some areas, Arctic fox predation on seal pups appears to be the major cause of pup mortality. Over the course of its evolution, however, the polar bear has become specialized for survival in a marine environment, and in terms of energy consumption, walking is about twice as costly for a polar bear as it is for a typical terrestrial mammal. This means that examining a number of seal dens before finding an occupied one is not the best hunting strategy for polar bears when alternatives exist.

Although polar bears do raid the birthing dens of ringed seals, particularly on land-fast ice in the

During open-sea seasons on Wrangel Island in the Siberian Arctic, many polar bears become stranded on the beach. They gather in large congregations of dozens of bears along the coastline, waiting until sea ice returns. During such times, the only available prey are walruses.

straits of archipelagos, their prime hunting habitats in the High Arctic are zones of active ice and the edges of ice floes. Here, using pressure ridges for cover, polar bears stalk immature, inexperienced seals that have been driven to these habitats from the more secure areas of land-fast ice by territorial adult male seals. Adolescent seals from six months to two years of age constitute the highest proportion of all ringed seals killed by polar bears.

Polar bears use two basic methods for hunting seals at dens. They locate an occupied den by scent and, perhaps, by sound. They then stalk their prey before charging forward and breaking through the snow roof to capture the seal within. Alternatively, they open a den and then wait until a seal comes to take a breath at the breathing hole under the den. If there are many dens close to each other, a bear will open all of them and then wait at one, often shading the gap in the roof with its head. When a seal comes to the surface, it does not realize that the den has been opened.

Waiting at the hole is called "still hunting." In summer, when seals haul out and bask in the sun on the ice, polar bears use the still-hunting technique along the edges of floes as well as at breathing holes. Still hunting requires a polar bear to be incredibly patient, but it uses less energy than more active methods of hunting. A polar bear lying at rest expends thirteen times less energy than it does when walking at an average speed of about 4 miles per hour (7 km/h).

Polar bears also stalk basking seals from underwater. They swim up to a seal's haul-out hole from beneath the ice, then charge onto the ice from the water or catch the seal as it slides into the water. Although seals are excellent swimmers, polar bears can even catch them in the water, but only beneath the ice, perhaps by using prominent parts of its undersurface as cover for stalking or by trapping the seal in narrow ice channels.

The bearded seal is larger than the ringed seal. An adult male may weigh up to 790 pounds (360 kg), with an average weight of 495 to 700 pounds (225–320 kg) and a body length of up to 8 feet (250 cm). Like ringed seals, bearded seals are true Arctic seals, inhabiting the entire circumpolar region during both summer and winter. Unlike ringed seals, they are bottom feeders, feeding on crustaceans, mollusks, worms, and fish such as Arctic cod. As bottom feeders, they are mainly found in the shallow regions of the continental shelf. Here they prefer active ice and the edges of ice floes, precisely the areas where most polar bears hunt. The world population of bearded seals is estimated to be between 200,000 and 300,000 animals.

Polar bears hunt bearded seals the same way they hunt ringed seals, except that bearded seals do not construct birthing dens. Adult polar bears of both sexes are efficient seal hunters, but larger and more powerful males tend to hunt bearded seals, and females concentrate their efforts on the smaller ringed seal.

When attacking walruses on the beach, polar bear males make riskier attacks than females. Males often try to seize even huge adult walrus, while females prudently focus their hunting mostly on calves.

Of the four seal species inhabiting the Arctic, the other two—the harp seal, *Phoca groenlandica,* and the hooded seal, *Cystophora cristata*—are limited to the Atlantic sector of the Arctic. They do not overwinter in the High Arctic, but migrate south in the autumn to subarctic regions. Both species are gregarious and live and hunt fish in the open sea. The females gather on the ice in huge numbers to give birth, particularly the harp seal whose maternity rookeries may comprise tens of thousands of individuals. The pups simply lie on the ice and are extremely vulnerable to predation. In the European part of their range, harp seals give birth in the White Sea, out of the range of polar bears. In the Canadian Arctic, however, polar bears may occasionally encounter harp seal rookeries. When this happens, the damage to the seal rookery may be considerable as the bear becomes excited and kills many more pups than it can eat. Such surplus slaughter may, however, be of benefit to the general polar bear population as other bears come in to scavenge on the remains.

The strength and hunting skills of polar bears allow them to hunt prey far larger than seals, and they have been known to attack and kill walruses and beluga whales. An adult female walrus can weigh up to 1,320 pounds (600 kg), the same as a beluga whale, but male walruses top the scales at up to 2,200

This adult male is eating a walrus calf that he robbed from a female bear after her successful hunting foray. Feeding upon each other's kills is a common habit among polar bears, although it is usually the kill made by an adult male that provides surplus food for the rest of polar bear community.

pounds (1,000 kg). Interactions between polar bears and walruses occur on the ice and on the shore when walruses haul out to form coastal rookeries. A few walruses remain in the High Arctic over the winter, staying in areas of open water. In such circumstances a narrow channel may freeze over while a walrus is sleeping on the ice, trapping it and making it easy prey for polar bears.

When live prey is not available, polar bears scavenge upon carrion. These two adult males examine walrus remains from previous years at a walrus haul-out site at Cape Blossom, Wrangel Island, in the Siberian Arctic.

Hunting walrus is a risky business for polar bears, and hunting success depends not only on the bear's strength, but also on its skill and intelligence. Walrus tusks are dangerous weapons, and a careless bear can be wounded or even killed. When they are hunting walruses on the beach, polar bears focus on calves. A female with cubs usually does not risk attacking as large and dangerous a prey as an adult walrus. An adult male bear may attempt to seize a mature walrus, but in the more than thirty walrus hunts I have observed on the beach, I have never seen a bear that could prevent even an exhausted adult walrus from escaping into the sea. On slippery ice, polar bears might have a better chance of stopping and killing an adult walrus.

Beluga whales become prey for polar bears when the whales swim deep into the ice fields, and the channels of open water are closed behind them by pressure or freezing. In such situations, dozens of belugas become crowded into small openings in the ice. Polar bears catch them and pull them out, killing as many as they can. At one such entrapment in the Bering Straits in the spring of 1984, over fifty beluga carcasses, mostly young animals, were observed on the ice with thirty polar bears feeding on them. Other records of Siberian polar bears hunting belugas are known from the southern part of the Chukchi Sea and in the Vilkitski Straits of the Kara Sea, indicating that such a situation is not unique. Polar bears catch narwhals, a less common Arctic whale about the same size as a beluga, in the same way.

Although polar bears are specialized predators, they are also opportunistic foragers who will scavenge on whale, walrus, and seal carcasses in addition to doing their own hunting. In areas where Arctic foxes hunt ringed seal pups, bears and foxes may exchange roles, with polar bears scavenging a fox kill if they find one. Polar bears must be adaptable to survive in their severe environment, and they hunt and consume anything edible if their preferred food is not available. When stranded on land, polar bears occasionally hunt musk oxen and small game such as voles, lemmings, ptarmigan, and geese. In autumn, when Arctic cod lay their eggs in the surf, polar bears collect fish that are thrown onto the beach by the waves. On Franz-Josef Land, even during the peak of their summer seal-hunting season, polar bears catch little auks, digging them from their nests beneath the rocks.

Polar bears have not totally relinquished the vegetarian tastes of their ancestors. Although hungry bears will eat kelp and any organic material they find on the beach, some consumption of plants is purely by choice. It is not unusual for polar bears to dive to get at algae on the sea bottom. Female polar bears eat considerable quantities of grass after emerging from their maternity dens in the spring, grazing for hours almost every day they remain within the denning area. It is thought the grass may serve to clean their digestive tracts after months of hibernation. Grazing, however, is not limited to springtime. Polar bears also eat grass while visiting the coasts of islands in the summer and autumn, perhaps not so much for calories as for the vitamins and minerals it contains. Whether or not the vegetation provides nutritional energy has yet to be studied; we do not know to what extent present-day polar bears have retained the physiological adaptations that allowed ancestral polar bears to utilize plant material. Whatever the case, plants do not constitute a large portion of the polar bear diet. By virtue of its power and skill, which eminently adapt it to its icy domain, the polar bear remains one of the world's super predators, a truly carnivorous bear.

Domains of Ice and Snow

The polar bear's domain encompasses the entire Arctic, expanding and contracting seasonally with the southern edge of the pack ice as it freezes southward in the winter and recedes north in the summer. The ice cap of the Arctic Ocean is not a solid plate, but a jumbled mass of ice structures of different ages, sizes, shapes, and densities. Changing winds and sea currents constantly wrench the ice sheets apart and then press them back together again, creating a variety of forms in the frozen seascape. The cap is an ice continent about 2,400 miles (4,000 km) in diameter with rugged ridges and vast plains of ice; long, winding leads as rivers; and polynya lakes and seas, all constantly moving and rotating around the North Pole. Patterns of ice-cover dynamics vary significantly in different regions of the Arctic and influence local spatial and temporal distributions and seasonal movements of polar bears.

The southernmost extent of the area permanently inhabited by polar bears reaches 50° N latitude in northeast Canada and 79° N near the western coast of Svalbard off the coast of Norway. To the north, the occasional bear may reach the North Pole; records have been made at 88° N and 89° N, and most recently, in 1996, at 89°30'. Although polar bears have been recorded 100 miles (160 km) inland, their highest densities are within the area of the Arctic continental shelf.

The continental shelf varies in width from 22 to 56 miles (37–93 km) in North America to over 900 miles (1,500 km) in the Barents Sea and covers more than one million square miles (2.5 million km²). The shallow waters of the continental shelf harbor very productive and diverse marine ecosystems, and biodiversity and productivity here is higher than in terrestrial ecosystems of the same region. In the Chukchi Sea, the edge of the continental shelf lies about 180 miles (300 km) north of Wrangel Island.

For a long time, polar bears were thought to travel without borders, drifting with the ice and wandering about the Arctic directed only by the availability of food. In the late 1960s, mark-and-recapture studies initiated in Canada, Svalbard, Greenland, and Alaska yielded the first evidence that polar bears may remain within restricted geographical areas, where their movements follow the seasonal changes in ice cover. Generally, in summer and autumn, polar bears concentrate at the edge of the pack ice, where their prey is

While walking, a polar bear appears to move slowly due to its "soft" body configuration combined with a gentleness and plasticity of movement. However, the image of a laggard is misleading; the animal can be quick in its actions and is able to cover surprisingly large distances in a short time.

most plentiful. As the ice cover solidifies and expands over the winter, polar bears disperse more widely.

According to the most recent estimates, a total of 21,000 to 28,000 polar bears inhabit the Arctic. Seventeen more or less distinct populations have been identified within the species' entire range. There are three populations in the Eurasian sector of the Arctic in the Eastern Hemisphere; thirteen in North America and Greenland in the Western Hemisphere; and one—the Chukchi Sea population—dissected by the 180th meridian and thus straddling both hemispheres. Estimates of polar bear numbers are approximate, as it is a challenging task to calculate the number of bears widely distributed over one of the world's most inaccessible regions.

Huge blocks of ice and ice ridges are not obstacles to a polar bear, but rather are useful features that help a bear to hide while stalking a seal.

The Chukchi Sea population inhabits the eastern part of the East Siberian Sea and the entire Chukchi Sea, expanding its range with the ice in winter to the northern part of the Bering Sea and the western part of the Beaufort Sea. Most bears from this population, possibly 80 percent of all breeding females, den on Wrangel and Herald Islands in the Russian sector of the Chukchi Sea. The population, estimated to be between 2,000 and 5,000 animals, appears to be stable or even increasing. The areas with the highest bear activity and concentrations include Wrangel and Herald Islands with their surrounding marine areas, as well as the central and southern parts of the Chukchi Sea. This population is considered to be a resource shared by Russia and the United States. Joint research projects on the Chukchi Sea bears are carried out by scientists from both countries, with shared conservation and management responsibilities to be fixed in an intergovernmental agreement following ongoing discussions.

The Laptev Sea population off the coast of central Siberia is the least studied and poorest known.

Opposite top: Coming out of the sea, a polar bear shakes water from its fur. Polar bears often then dry their fur by crawling in the snow.
Opposite bottom: In the water, polar bears are as confident as they are on ice, proving they are true marine animals. During their wanderings over drifting ice, they often have to swim across polynyas and leads, and are known to swim for up to 70 miles (120 km) in the open sea. They also swim and dive while stalking seals, and often escape from danger into the sea.

Sea of
Okhotsk

Bering
Sea

RUSSIA

East Siberian
Sea

Laptev
Sea

Chukchi
Sea

Wrangel
Island

Herald
Island

Karaskoye More

Gulf of
Alaska

USA

Arctic
Ocean

Pacific
Ocean

Beaufort
Sea

Barents
Sea

North
Pole

CANADA

Baffin
Bay

Greenland
Sea

Norwegian
Sea

Denmark
Strait

North
Sea

Hudson
Bay

Davis
Strait

Atlantic
Ocean

Southernmost border of regular polar bear meetings

Northern and southermost regions of high density polar bear populations

● Remote sightings of polar bears

Bears of this population inhabit the western part of the East Siberian Sea, the eastern part of the Kara Sea, and the entire Laptev Sea, including the New Siberian Islands, Severnaya Zemlya, and the northern coast of the Taimyr Peninsula. Major denning areas are on the New Siberian Islands and Severnaya Zemlya. A very rough estimate of this population's size is 800 to 1,200 animals.

Preliminary estimates for the size of the Franz-Josef Land–Novaya Zemlya population on the European side of the Russian Arctic coastline are 2,500 to 3,500 bears, spread over the eastern part of the Barents Sea and Franz-Josef Land, Novaya Zemlya, and the western part of the Kara Sea. Prime denning habitats are on the eastern coast of Novaya Zemlya and Franz-Josef Land.

Arctic foxes are the only other terrestrial mammal that penetrates into the Arctic pack ice as far as polar bears do. On the ice, Arctic foxes often follow polar bears to feed upon remains of the bears' kills.

Although some polar bears travel between Svalbard off the coast of Norway and Franz-Josef Land, satellite-telemetry tracking by Norwegian researchers since the 1970s has shown that the ranges of Svalbard bears are mostly restricted to Svalbard and the western Barents Sea region. Due to this finding, this population, estimated at 1,700 to 2,200 animals, is now considered distinct.

There are more distinct populations of polar bears in North America than there are in Siberia and the European Arctic, although this may reflect the extent of the research that has been carried out in the Canadian Arctic and Alaska rather than major differences in the distribution of bears. In the Canadian Arctic archipelago, polar bears tend to live around certain straits, sounds, and bays, as well as on particular islands. Twelve distinct populations have been identified: East Greenland (2,000 to 4,000 bears); Southeast Baffin Island (950 bears); Lancaster Sound and North Baffin Bay (2,470 bears); Fox Basin (2,020 bears); Eastern Hudson Bay (1,000 bears); Western Hudson Bay (1,200 bears); Gulf of Boothia (900 bears); M'Clintock Channel (700 bears); Viscount Melville Sound (230 bears); North Beaufort Sea (1,200 bears); South Beaufort Sea (1,800 bears), and Northwest Greenland and Ellesmere Island (population size unknown).

The polar bears of Hudson Bay in Canada are the southernmost population of this species in the world. They are unique in the dynamics of their spatial distribution: Every year as all the ice melts in Hudson Bay, the entire population is forced to spend four months on land, from July until November, behaving like true—but temporary—terrestrial bears. This is the time when they have to live on kelp and other vegetation, and hunt birds and rodents. Only when the bay begins to freeze do the bears from this population return to the ice to hunt seals again.

Although polar bears are not migratory animals, their seasonal movements in some areas may be considerable. In the Beaufort Sea, for example, they move up to 390 miles (650 km) in an east-west direction and 145 miles (240 km) in a north-south direction. Bears from the Chukchi Sea population, which spend the winter in the north Bering Sea, move with the receding ice in the spring to the central Chukchi Sea, traveling hundreds of miles before moving back to the Bering Sea in autumn.

How far an individual bear may wander depends on ice conditions and the availability of prey. During the year, a bear may cover a home range of from 24,000 to more than 120,000 square miles (60,000–300,000 km^2), walking at an average speed of 2.7 miles per hour (4.5 km/h). Females accompanied by cubs less than a year old adjust their speed to their cubs' abilities, normally walking no faster than 1.5 to 2.4 miles per hour (2.5–4 kph). Polar bears can run as fast as 24 miles per hour (40 kph), but only over short distances as they easily become overheated. If chased, polar bears can run for a mile or two (a few kilometers) at speeds of 12 to 18 miles per hour (20–30 kph), and then switch to a fast walking rate of 4.8 to 6 miles per hour (8–10 kph). Even slowing its pace, an adult bear cannot run for more than 4.8 to 6 miles (8–10 km). Young bears run with less effort and can cover up to 9 miles (15 km) without stopping.

Although the majority of marked bears show fidelity to their home ranges, exceptions are known. In North America, for example, one tagged bear was killed 1,930 miles (3,218 km) from where he had been captured a year earlier. In most species males are more mobile than females, and there is no reason to expect that polar bears are much different. Perhaps if we were able to provide more male polar bears with satellite transmitters, our present understanding of polar bear fidelity to particular regions might have to be corrected.

Opposite top: Narrow leads across solid plates of plain ice are places where seals haul out, and polar bears never pass such leads without examination.
Opposite bottom: Walking at an average speed of 2.7 miles per hour (4.5 km/h), a polar bear can cover tens of miles in a single day. As with most mammal species, polar bear males cover more ground than females.

Polar Bear Seasons

Winter in the High Arctic is a mysterious time. Even at the highest latitudes, the polar night does not pass in total darkness. In clear, frosty weather cold flames of the aurora borealis, the northern lights, play in the dark sky, illuminating shadowy silhouettes on the ice below. When the moon appears, everything takes on a surreal green cast, and landscape features can be seen from miles away. Although many creatures leave in the autumn for lower latitudes, winter is not a dead season in the High Arctic. Life goes on not only beneath the sea ice, but on the surface as well. Openings in the ice cover provide life support for gulls, guillemots, seals, walruses, narwhals, and belugas. For Ivory and Ross' gulls, wintering in the High Arctic is their normal way of life. While other birds migrate south, these small, graceful gulls move northward to meet the darkness of the polar night. Many Arctic foxes move north as well, where they survive on the ice by scavenging polar bear kills.

Polar bears do not stop hunting even during the most severe winter months. Only pregnant females spend the winter in snow dens, where, during December and January—the darkest months of the polar night—they give birth to a new generation of polar bears. Pregnant females spend about 160 to 170 days in maternity dens from October to March or April. Other bears go into dens only when conditions are especially harsh and no prey is available, sleeping a much shorter time than females in maternity dens. Probably more bears at higher latitudes (other than pregnant females) spend part of the winter in sleep than bears in southern areas. In northern Taimyr, for example, young bears and adult males stay in dens up to 52 days a year, females with yearlings sleep up to 106 days, and females without cubs remain dormant as long as 125 days. Occasional observations on winter denning of lone bears or females with yearlings have been made in the Canadian Arctic and Greenland, but never in Alaska.

Polar bear sleep is not true hibernation. In the true hibernation of marmots, ground squirrels, and some species of bat, the animal's body temperature drops to 32.5 to 34.7 degrees Fahrenheit (1°–5° C), breathing and heart rate are severely reduced, and the animal's metabolism drops twenty to forty fold.

Acquaintance with the world begins for polar bear cubs in early spring, when their mother opens her maternity den for the first time. When they emerge from the den, cubs are not well insulated from cold, so they often press against their mother's thick fur to stay warm and safe.

In this state of deep torpor even a strong outside stimulus such as a loud noise or pain does not wake the animal up. Hibernation for polar bears is more accurately a state of deep sleep. While sleeping in their dens, polar bears maintain a slightly reduced body temperature of 51.4 to 52.5 degrees Fahrenheit (35°–37° C), their heart rate gradually drops from 60 to 27 beats per minute and becomes irregular, and their breathing rate slows to 2.5 to 3.5 times a minute. In this condition bears are easily awakened, and females can take care of their cubs if necessary.

The polar bear mating season begins in early April and continues through May. During courtship, polar bear pairs constantly move, cover long distances, and are difficult to track and observe. These two young bear males demonstrate a sequence of sexual behavior while playing in autumn on shore; this is not true copulation, although it looks exactly like it.

Female polar bears give birth to their young on land in maternity dens made in the snow. Only polar bears from the Beaufort Sea population den on the ice; more than half of the dens in this population are constructed on pack ice and some are constructed on land-fast ice. The majority of pregnant females from the Chukchi-Alaskan population come to Wrangel and Herald Islands to make their dens. A polar bear's maternity den is a comfortable dwelling beneath the snow. Usually it has one chamber, which varies from 40 to 200 inches (100–510 cm) in length, 28 to 156 inches (70–390 cm) in width, and 12 to 76 inches (30–190 cm) in height, but some dens have more than one chamber. The main chamber is connected to the surface by a tunnel from 6 inches to 27 feet (15–820 cm) long. Despite the great variety of maternity den sizes and shapes, they all share one important feature—the entrance is always lower than the chamber.

Snow density and thickness are the most important factors in maintaining optimal conditions inside the den. Usually the chamber is separated from the outside environment by a layer of snow 12 to 40 inches (30–100 cm) thick. During the winter the den entrance is closed by snow. Temperatures inside the den are about 43 degrees Fahrenheit (20° C) higher than the outside temperature. Measurements taken on Wrangel Island revealed that while the outside air temperature fluctuated between 24 to 17 degrees

Fahrenheit (-14° to -27° C), inside the den the temperature remained between 28 and 35 degrees Fahrenheit (-5.6° to +6° C) in different parts of the den.

While they are sleeping in their maternity dens, females do not eat or drink; they live entirely off their fat deposits. During the winter, they give birth to one, two, or, rarely, three cubs each weighing about 1.3 to 1.7 pounds (0.6–0.8 kg). Polar bear milk is very rich. With 31 percent fat and 10.2 percent protein, it is similar in composition to seal and whale milk. On this diet the cubs grow quickly and, over the course of five to six months, increase their weight by a factor of 15 to 25, usually leaving the den weighing 17.6 to 33 pounds (8–15 kg). By the end of the denning period, the larger cubs have become more active inside the den, and the females accommodate them by enlarging the chamber.

Polar bears emerge from their dens when spring comes to the Arctic. The first signs that a female is ready to come out are a few small pieces of snow visible on an otherwise unblemished wind-blown slope. The female pushes these pieces out of the entrance's snow cover to make an air hole. She may make this small initial opening to monitor outside conditions or to gradually accustom her cubs to the cold. For a few days no further changes indicate the bear family's presence. Then, all of a sudden, blocks of snow are pushed out from below, and a black nose appears in the entrance. The nose tests the air for a few minutes. Only then will the female show herself.

Quietly sitting at the maternity den entrance in the late evening sun, this mother with her single cub looks out over her denning area. After emerging from the den, females normally do not leave for the ice immediately, but stay within the denning area for a period of from two weeks to a month, waiting until their cubs grow strong enough to travel in the harsh sea-ice environment.

Usually the first exit hole is narrow, and the female has to force herself through it, sometimes twisting like a corkscrew as she pushes her way out. First of all, she sits down at the entrance and surveys her surroundings. Only after she has assured herself that there is nothing dangerous in the den's vicinity will she slide down the slope, swimming and rolling in the snow to clean her fur. She obviously enjoys these activities after being confined for months in the den's narrow chamber. After cleaning her fur, the female heads to a valley or terrace. There she digs through the snow and eats grass, like a cow grazing in a meadow.

The time of den emergence and departure for the ice depends on the condition of both the female and her cubs. If the female is fat enough, she may stay in the denning area for two to three weeks, or as long as a month if she is not disturbed. Only thin females leave the denning area soon after emergence. Small cubs may not follow their mother on her first excursion, but if she wants them to follow, she will call them, turning to face the entrance and making a soft "coughing" sound.

After emergence, the female makes one or more day beds within the family's temporary home range in the denning area. A polar bear day bed is a hole about 1.5 to 5 feet (0.5–1.5 m) deep and from 3 to 6.5 feet (1–2 m) wide dug in the snow. One of these day beds is usually 65 to 100 feet (20–30 m) from the maternity den. Sometimes females who have emerged with cubs make deeper holes, developing one or more day beds into temporary dens. If undisturbed, females usually spend calm, sunny days outside, basking in the sun or taking their cubs for short walks. They lead them back into the maternity den only when forced inside by a cold wind or a blizzard.

If the cubs are not sleeping or nursing, they are playing. They are so joyful and self-abandoned in play that watching them is an exhilarating spiritual experience. Their play is a continuous cascade of play fights, somersaults, toboggan runs, and chases after pieces of snow. Cubs can play without a break for half an hour or more. These periods of play seem to be important for preparing the cubs for their life on the ice. With every excursion, the cubs become stronger, and their locomotive skills develop. When they first emerge from the den, the cubs crawl on their bellies like reptiles, but after just a few days outside they can walk, run, and jump, and climb up steep slopes and scramble over rocks in pursuit of their mother.

Polar bear females are conscientious mothers. They are gentle and careful but strict if necessary. If her cubs misbehave, a polar bear mother disciplines them by pressing them to the ground with her jaws or by nipping them. Perhaps conscious of small cubs' extreme vulnerability during their first weeks outside the den, a polar bear mother is particularly sensitive to any disturbance. If a female merely suspects a threat, the whole family returns to the den and hides. A pronounced disturbance, such as a snowmobile driving through the denning area, may have serious consequences. The most nervous females may leave their dens immediately and lead their cubs away, even if the cubs are very young and unprepared to travel.

Sea of
Okhotsk

Bering
Sea

RUSSIA

East Siberian
Sea

Laptev
Sea

Chukchi
Sea

Wrangel
Island

Herald
Island

Karaskoye More

Gulf of
Alaska

USA

Arctic
Ocean

Pacific
Ocean

Beaufort
Sea

North
Pole

Barents
Sea

CANADA

Greenland
Sea

Baffin
Bay

Norwegian
Sea

Denmark
Strait

North
Sea

Hudson
Bay

Davis
Strait

Atlantic
Ocean

Polar Bear denning sites

One day a mother bear simply decides it is time to lead her family away from the denning area. She and her cubs head out on a routine walk and do not return. Other dens become important for the family while the cubs become conditioned for more extensive travels. In areas with a high density of dens, experienced females usually move with their cubs from one den to another, entering dens abandoned by the original occupants. Females may even compete for dens that for some reason seem to be more attractive than others. At this stage the cubs have grown enough to take another step toward maturity: It is time for them to learn how the scents of other bears differ from that of their mother.

March and April are the months when ringed seals give birth to their young. These are also the months when polar bear females start breaking out from their maternity dens, which means that hunting conditions are favorable when the mothers head out onto the ice with their cubs. It is time for the cubs to try seal meat and to start learning the skills necessary for independent survival in their unpredictable and unforgiving environment.

Spring is also the time when adult male polar bears begin their search for mates. The first females to come into estrous are those without cubs. If a mother loses her cubs by accident, she will come into estrous that same spring, but a little later in the season. A female with cubs does not become receptive until her cubs are weaned, normally when the cubs are two and a half years old. Males and females will court from as early as March and continue as late as June. The peak of the mating season is in late April and May.

Usually a female will have her first cubs when she is six or seven years old, although some females become sexually mature as young as four. A female reaches the peak of her reproductive potential between ten and nineteen years of age, and may continue to have cubs until she is twenty-one. During her life a female may produce six to seven litters, or about ten to fifteen cubs. Males may be capable of fathering cubs as early as three years of age, but are not full grown until they are about eight to ten years old. In captivity males have mated successfully between the ages of three and nineteen. In the wild, due to the considerable difference in size between younger and older males and competition for females, it is unlikely that young males have the opportunity to mate until they are at least six years old.

Receptive females mark blocks of snow or other prominent objects with urine; males detect females by scent and follow them. It is not unusual for more than one male to find a receptive female, as neither sex is territorial and both range widely over the ice. In such situations males fight each other for the right to mate, and these altercations often result in serious wounds and broken canine teeth.

An established pair stays together for ten to twelve days, copulating several times a day. This frequent stimulation is necessary to induce the release of an egg in the female (ovulation). Courting polar bears are rarely observed in the wild, and a sequence of copulations has been observed only once—near Wrangel Island. The sequence consisted of three instances of copulation lasting three, seven, and ten minutes respectively. In April 1993, I observed a pair of courting and copulating bears on the ice near Herald Island, but the bears were too far away for me to record any details. Part of the problem is that courting bears do not stay in any one place for more than a few hours, perhaps to avoid unwanted interactions with competing males.

A mated pair walks together. The animals touch one another often and lick each other's faces. They play on the ice, rolling and leaping in the snow. Mating during one season, however, may not be restricted to a single partner; one male may copulate with more than one female (polygamy), and the same is true for females (polyandry). Almost nothing is known about the strength of social bonds between sexual partners. Until now, there has been only one piece of evidence that the same partners may get together again in subsequent years. One spring in Svalbard, a female marked with a transmitter mated with a marked male. Three years later they were seen together again at the female's next estrous cycle.

Eggs fertilized in the spring do not implant and begin to develop until September or October, when the female comes ashore to den. Because of this delayed implantation, the gestation period in polar bears is 195 to 265 days. Delayed implantation ensures that the cubs are born in snow dens, protected from the harsh conditions of winter, and allows the females the summer to hunt to build up the supplies of fat they need to produce milk for their young.

All polar bears prefer to spend the summer away from land and out on the ice. During the summer, prey is plentiful but not always easily available. As the sea ice melts and recedes to the north, the movements of the broken ice fields left behind are unpredictable. Wildlife concentrates along the edge of the more reliable, solid pack ice, and this is where most polar bears, especially females with cubs less than a year old, prefer to hunt. Lone young bears and adult males may pursue more adventurous hunting strategies in the broken peripheral ice fields.

As the ice recedes, polar bears either have to move north with their prey or swim south to the nearest land. In extreme situations when the ice recedes far from land, polar bears are forced to stay on shore for weeks. When this happens, polar bears live mostly off their fat deposits, using the reserves they have built up for winter. As soon as the ice returns, the bears move out onto the frozen sea to continue hunting. Late autumn and the first half of the winter can be the most difficult times of year for the bears because weather conditions are particularly harsh with blizzards following one after another, and the ice is unstable, making hunting difficult.

During the short summer season, polar bears of both sexes and all ages have to prepare for winter. Bear mothers have to acquire twice the amount of food as a lone bear. When they emerge from their dens in the spring they weigh about 395 to 660 pounds (180–300 kg). They hunt constantly during the summer to increase their weight to 770 to 880 pounds (350–400 kg), if they are lucky, and they also have to provide for their cubs. In successful families, by early September the young cubs are so plump they look like large fur balls.

The first pregnant females come ashore in late August, and more arrive in September and October. By the end of October the snow cover is usually thick enough for most mothers-to-be to have settled into maternity dens for hibernation. Those who arrived earliest may have had to wait weeks for sufficient snow cover to excavate a den. The bears lie down in places where they expect a good cover of snow to form, but they do not, as is sometimes reported, simply wait until the snow covers them. When a layer of snow accumulates, a mother bear actively searches for a suitable denning area, sometimes digging up to fifteen test holes until she finally settles on one. If disturbed at a den she has prepared, a female leaves and usually does not return to the same spot.

If all goes well, pregnant females find safe, secure locations to pass the High Arctic winter. As the bitter cold winds scour the seemingly lifeless slopes above the maternity dens, the latest generation of polar bears—and the species' best assurance for survival—is slowly developing in the quiet warmth of a mother's care.

Polar bear females are excellent, selfless mothers. Normally, cubs stay under their mother's care for two and half years, learning from her hunting and survival skills. Even when shot and injured, polar bear mothers do not leave cubs, staying with them to the end.

A Social Interlude

The private life of the polar bear is the most puzzling and exciting aspect of the species' biology. Social behavior among polar bears might seem to be a contradiction in terms. A species that spends most of its life wandering alone over thousands of miles of shifting sea ice can hardly be thought to have any social skills. Yet polar bears do gather in concentrations of up to a hundred or more, usually at a significant source of food such as a whale carcass or a walrus rookery. They need behavioral mechanisms to cope on these and other occasions when circumstances change the pattern of their otherwise solitary existence.

The study of social behavior in polar bears presents numerous challenges to the researcher. Modern technology is no substitute for firsthand observation, and academic training must be supplemented by a passion for observing polar bears in their natural environment. Add to that the near impossibility of predicting where polar bears will gather. If the researcher is lucky enough to detect the animals before they disperse, there are usually no facilities close at hand to facilitate any observations. Polar bears can be observed from cliffs edging the shorelines of Arctic islands, but the bears usually do not remain in sight long enough for researchers to record anything more than fragmentary images of their interactions. There are, however, two places in the world where polar bears gather with some regularity—Wrangel Island in the Chukchi Sea and Cape Churchill on Hudson Bay in northern Canada. I have had the privilege to observe polar bears in both places.

On Wrangel Island, large coastal congregations of polar bears form in autumns when the ocean is ice free, usually every two to five years. During my four seasons of autumn observations of bears on Wrangel, I have watched and recorded 186 social interactions between polar bears of both sexes and all ages in a variety of situations. Anywhere from 12 to 150 bears might gather near a walrus rookery, at a walrus carcass, or around a beached whale. In addition to these large gatherings, bears wandered individually or in small groups over the beach and nearby tundra. Under such circumstances a density of 62 to 95 bears per acre (25–38 bears per ha) was not unusual.

Polar bears are among the most playful animals on Earth. These two young males are completely preoccupied with play fighting; they may continue to wrestle for hours until they are totally exhausted.

My first surprise was that the bears appeared to be very tolerant of each other while they were gathered together on shore. Even though social distance is an important component of animal behavior— and all polar bears take care to follow the rules of social etiquette—I did not find any spatial separation between males and females with young or between young and adult bears. I found this astonishing. Aggression by adult male polar bears toward family groups and younger bears is thought to be common and one reason why family groups avoid being in areas occupied by adult male polar bears; however, I never observed this type of avoidance either on Wrangel or at Cape Churchill. Females with cubs gathered in the same areas as lone bears of all ages and both sexes.

Polar bears have well-developed patterns of communicative behavior that are expressive enough for even a human to understand. These behaviors are effective tools for avoiding serious conflicts. In addition to these formal behaviors, a bear's personality and intelligence are important factors in managing social interactions and establishing an individual bear's position within the temporary community. Each individual reacts differently depending on the situation and on the experience and maturity of the animal.

Polar bears are powerful animals; however, fights in which blood is spilled are restricted to specific situations, such as competition between males in the spring for receptive females. Even then polar bears normally do not fight to the death. In general, I found that individuals in polar bear communities were less aggressive than individuals in communities of many other non-predatory species, such as snow geese or walruses. According to most books and films about polar bears, mothers with cubs avoid adult males because the males prey on cubs. In fact, only a few instances have ever been reported of males killing cubs, and even those few cases are suspect—if a bear is observed eating the carcass of another bear, it does not necessarily mean it killed the bear. In all species, young animals usually lose aggressive interactions with adults, and it is natural for mothers to protect their young against possible risk. Based on the observations collected to date, we have no reason to believe that males are a significant factor in cub mortality.

My observations on Wrangel revealed that females with cubs were the most aggressive individuals in the polar bear community. Often a female would bite an adult male or strike him with her forepaw during an aggressive charge, but instead of retaliating, the male always retreated. Once on Cape Churchill I observed an irate female with two two-year-old cubs. She was so determined to push away a huge adult

Polar bear play fight is a ballet of pushing, striking, hugging, jumping on each other, and romping in snow. As with other animals, play behavior is an important mean of establishing social bonds between individual polar bears. Playmates are not necessarily bears of the same sex and age.

male that had come too close to her family that she attacked him five times in succession. The fifth time, while striking at him with her forepaw, she lost her balance and fell down onto the snow. Even then the male did not press his advantage. He merely opened his mouth as he tried to fend her off while taking a few steps backward.

In contrast to the low proportion of aggressive displays I observed, expressions of social tolerance (close proximity to each other without avoidance or aggression) constituted a much larger part of social events—just under one-third of all interactions I observed. Mature females with one- or two-year-old cubs typically group together when approached by another bear. In such situations younger, less experienced females with cubs less than a year old prefer to retreat. Polar bears also group together, at least temporarily, when they are exposed to danger. In Canada adult males were observed forming a group when an airplane flew overhead. On Wrangel Island, bears of different ages and both sexes grouped together when they ran away from me along the gravel spit or into the sea.

Polar bears often group together closely enough to establish physical contact. This happened in one-fifth of all the observations I recorded on Wrangel. On the shore in autumn, adult males seem to actively seek out the company of other males. Their mutual attraction results in what I call "male rookeries," in which males come together at day-bed sites, usually lying 3 to 10 feet (1–3 m) from each other and sometimes even touching. Pairs of male bears in these groupings often behaved as though they were friends, walking or playing together. Such alliances appear to be more than accidental; a pair may separate for some time, but then the same bears join up again. Bonds become even more obvious when friends refuse to accept another individual into their company.

The basic social units in polar bear populations are mothers with cubs. We do not know, however, how long familial bonds between individual bears are maintained, nor whether friendships between individual, unrelated males are an indication that polar bear communities are more complex than we think. At least one group of bears I observed seemed to be an extended family. In the autumn of 1991, in a coastal congregation of polar bears on Wrangel Island, I observed a group of four bears. A mother and her two two-year-old cubs were accompanied by another adult female, apparently younger than the mother but obviously older than the cubs. These four bears remained together for more than a month, sleeping together on one day bed and acting as a family unit in all social situations.

Polar bears are not territorial and do not defend food resources, but they may compete for a particular item of food or for a place at a carcass. A stronger bear may take a kill away from a weaker hunter, but at the same time, it is usual for several polar bears to feed simultaneously from a single carcass. Furthermore, it is the rule rather than the exception that if a carcass is available, every bear that finds it can get a place at the feast. I have observed as many as fourteen bears eating shoulder to shoulder from the carcass of a rather small walrus calf. Although there is always a lot of growling and lunging with open mouths during such shared meals, bears that have already gorged themselves do not object to other bears joining them, especially if the newcomers approach gently and insert themselves into the group with proper decorum. Special behavior to solicit food or a place at a carcass includes a slow, docile approach with the body pressed low to the ground, circling around, and touching noses. Bears of either sex may find themselves begging for food from others, and the supplicant is usually rewarded with a meal.

Polar bear hierarchy is relative and depends on the current mood of the animals and how strongly motivated they are in different situations. A general rule is that a direct approach is always a threat, regardless of the size or power of the approaching individual. Although females with cubs are not generally subordinate to adult males, who are often rather shy and easily frightened, they usually do not risk approaching stronger adult males. The larger the individual the more confident he is, and the more respect and attention he commands from others.

Subadult bears—yearlings and two-year-olds—are lower in the social hierarchy, and their rank depends on whether or not they are still with their mothers. Most cubs remain under their mothers' protection until they are two and a half years old, but some are weaned in their second year. Such subadults are at the bottom of the scale, dominated both by adult bears and by subadults still accompanied by their mothers.

Mothers with cubs tolerate other mothers with cubs at much closer distances than they tolerate lone bears, perhaps understanding that mothers share similar problems and would not hurt one another's offspring. Females with cubs and young bears maintain greater distances from other bears in general, usually at least 50 to 115 feet (15–35 m), and both groups are particularly watchful of large males.

A mother and her two-year-old cubs pile on top of each other while resting in the snow. Sleeping in physical contact with one another helps polar bears reduce heat loss—and is also important in a social context as a form of integrating within a group.

Polar bears are more confident out on the ice than they are on land as out on the ice they can escape into the sea at any sign of danger. As soon as the ocean begins to freeze in the autumn, they scatter widely over the Arctic pack. Away from land and back in their natural environment, their social distance increases, and they become more suspicious of one another. Despite the change in conditions, however, out on the ice they maintain loose contact with others of their kind. They follow each other's tracks, scavenge each other's kills, and orient to one another following the simple rule that if there are polar bears somewhere, something of interest is happening there. Even while living out their lives as solitary predators of the Arctic pack ice, they remain the most social bears on Earth.

Polar bears are intelligent and inquisitive animals. Scouting along deserted Arctic coasts, a bear would not pass a remote cabin without examining it. It is curiosity, not aggression or hunting motivation, that led this bear to look through the window into the author's cabin in the Siberian Arctic.

Encountering Polar Bears

Experienced Arctic explorers and hunters know that polar bears generally pose no threat to people. Despite their size and power, polar bears are calm, cautious, and rather timid animals. Even when they have been wounded by hunters, polar bears are normally not aggressive. In former times, indigenous northern people hunted polar bears with spears and bows and arrows, and old Chukchi hunters knew that a simple wooden stick would provide protection against a polar bear. In contrast to this practical knowledge gained through centuries of interaction between polar bears and humans, fear and ignorance drive the imagination and behavior of today's inexperienced visitor to the polar bear's realm.

Conflicts between humans and polar bears do occur, but accidents in which people are injured or killed by bears are rare and, more often than not, provoked by the human side of the equation. When polar bears and people meet, it is usually the bears that are at risk. On the island of Novaya Zemlya off the western coast of Siberia, only two or three polar bear attacks on humans have been reported for the past one hundred years. On Wrangel Island, where polar bear density is one of the highest known for the world, hunters have killed thousands of polar bears, but not a single person has ever been killed or even injured by a bear. Based on an analysis of available records, Professor Savva Uspenski of the Russian Institute of Nature Conservation (formerly the All-Union Institute of Nature Conservation) in Moscow reported that from 1930 to 1968—the time of the most intensive exploration in the Russian Arctic—not more than ten people were killed or injured by polar bears.

Conflicts between polar bears and people generally occur in three types of situations: when polar bears approach human settlements (polar weather stations, research stations on drifting pack ice, trappers' cabins, or, more rarely, coastal villages), when polar bears come across people working in the tundra close to the coast, and when people deliberately approach polar bears or their dens.

The first type of situation is the one most likely to be fatal to the bear. Polar bears are inquisitive animals, and it is natural for them to approach and investigate anything they come across in their travels, especially if food is involved—either cached in a cabin or tossed in a garbage dump. They can be very persistent in breaking through any barrier that stands between them and food, whether the barrier is a door, a wall, or a window. Dogs can also be an attraction. Although most bears are frightened away by dogs, a few may kill and eat them. In the Russian Arctic, a typical precursor to conflict is the feeding of polar bears at polar weather stations. Baited bears lose their fear of people; they become accustomed to staying around camps and may attempt to "knock" food out of a person if the opportunity arises.

If there is no food around, polar bears are usually very gentle while investigating human property. When I was living in a remote cabin on Wrangel Island, polar bears approached my camp a total of 149

Designed for viewing polar bears, this famous camp I set up at Cape Churchill, Manitoba, Canada, is the only place in the world where people can watch polar bear behavior in their natural environment—and still enjoy the living facilities of modern civilization.

times during four autumn seasons, sometimes as often as five times a day. The visitors never tried to break any part of the cabin or any of my belongings. Only once did a very thin and evidently hungry young female bite the wooden frame of the cabin window, perhaps catching the scent of my supper through the frame. She did not respond when I knocked against the inside wall, and I had to go outside and pretend that I intended to attack her in order to drive her away. In most cases, polar bears that visit human dwellings run off as soon as they realize that people are present.

Mothers with cubs may be dangerous if they come across people unexpectedly, as the mother bears may decide to defend their offspring rather than run away. It is easy to avoid these situations by getting in the habit of checking for bears before stepping out of a vehicle or shelter in the Arctic.

If a polar bear meets a person out on the tundra or along the coast, in most cases the scent or sight of a human is enough to scare the bear away immediately. Occasionally, a bear might decide to have a closer look and approach to within a few yards before it recognizes the presence of a human being and flees. The natural reaction of a person approached by a polar bear is to retreat nervously, which unfortunately encourages the inquisitive bear to follow. Young, inexperienced bears may be less careful in such situations and, if provoked, may cause an unwanted encounter. The best thing a person can do is to step

An adult male examines cavities between ice blocks for signs of a seal's presence. Polar bears can detect the smell of their marine-mammal prey from tens of miles away. This is why they often visit sealers' and whalers' camps and native people's settlements, exposing themselves to the risk of being shot.

confidently away from the bear so as not to appear to be running away, and, if possible, to get upwind of the bear so that it can catch the person's scent. In extreme situations, it might be necessary to simulate an attack on the bear to get it to move away. Only a bear that has been habituated to the presence of people—for instance, by associating people with food—would stand its ground in the face of such an attack.

Polar bears and people also interact when people come to polar bear dens. A female disturbed at her den usually either hides quietly in the den or makes threatening gestures from inside her temporary home. For many years, scientific researchers routinely surveyed polar bear dens on Wrangel Island in the spring, and only rarely did a female come out of her den to scare away an intruder. The researchers were never hurt in these encounters, but the mother bears often abandoned their dens afterwards, even if their cubs were very young.

Data from the Norwegian archipelago of Svalbard, where record keeping on polar bear–human conflicts has been more comprehensive than in the Russian Arctic, tells us much about the fate of polar bears when they meet up with people. During the fourteen years from 1973 to 1987, a total of forty-seven cases of polar bears threatening people, dogs, or property were recorded. Forty-six of these situations resulted in the bear being shot dead; in the remaining case a wounded bear escaped. During the same fourteen-year period, two people were injured and one man was killed, but the bears involved were not shot. Most polar bears, it seems, were shot while they were visiting human settlements, not when they were attacking people. The problem managing interactions with polar bears is that in most cases people do not understand bear behavior and misinterpret curiosity as aggressive intent. This means that many polar bears are killed merely because they are being curious.

There had been no attempts to analyze polar bear behavioral patterns during interactions with human beings until I started interacting with the bears on Wrangel Island in September 1990. During four seasons, I recorded 492 direct encounters with bears. Over three-quarters of the interactions occurred away from the cabin; one-quarter occurred near the cabin—sometimes even in the doorway or outer room of the cabin, where the bears liked to investigate when the door was open.

The most typical reaction was for the bear to retreat as soon as it had visually identified me, usually at a distance of between 100 and 990 feet (30–300 m). This happened just over 60 percent of the time.

Ten percent of the time, the mere scent of me would be enough to make the bear run away. Of the 192 direct interactions, on only five occasions did polar bears display an approach other than the usual slow, nervous advance to a distance of 10 to 33 feet (3–10 m), followed by the bear's retreat. These more threatening displays involved hissing, snorting, and, in a few cases, gnashing of teeth. In four of these five interactions the bear made an attack display—a short rapid run toward me—before suddenly stopping a few yards away. In only one instance was there a serious intent to attack, and this came from a female protecting her cubs. The mother bear wanted to drive me away from a gravel spit where she had settled to rest, and she charged three times to within three feet (1 m) of where I was standing. She stopped each time, however, when I hit the ground in front of her with a pole and then aimed the end of the pole at her face, using the pole the way a walrus uses its tusks to fend off a polar bear attack.

Even though they are the world's largest terrestrial predator, polar bears have still not lost their caution. To survive, any wild animal has to be careful within its physical and social environment, and polar bears are no exception.

Polar bears are afraid of people not because people are relatively large or because they have had unpleasant encounters with them, but because polar bears tend to be cautious about all new creatures they meet—even small ones. More than once on Wrangel Island I observed polar bears become nervous and frightened if a snowy owl landed nearby or if an Arctic fox trotted past. Once I watched an adult male polar bear terribly frightened by three ravens. The polar bear was walking along the beach of a lagoon. He came around a corner to see three ravens jumping up and down. There was no food around and the birds were probably just playing. The bear was so startled that he ran headlong into the water and dived through the frozen slush of the lagoon, breaking his way through the icy mass to get to the other side. He continued his mad dash on the other side of the lagoon, disappearing on the seaward side of the gravel spit. The ravens did not pay much attention to this timid giant and barely paused in their play. To a scavenger, it seems, a polar bear is nothing more than a meal ticket.

A Fragile Giant

Perfectly adapted to its harsh environment, the polar bear remained unthreatened in its Arctic stronghold until the ambitions and greed of the civilized world shattered the equilibrium of the North. Early native peoples harvested polar bears for subsistence, and their traditional uses hardly affected bear populations. Their take was limited by their primitive hunting tools, the low density of their settlements, and their inability to penetrate deep into the ice. In the sixteenth century, European explorers came to the Arctic in search of new trade routes around the world and stayed to exploit its riches. They brought with them firearms and a desire to gain dominion over all they saw.

The history of Arctic exploration was in large part the history of Arctic conquest, and foremost among the wildlife victims of this conquest was the polar bear. The same habits and characteristics that permit polar bears to survive on the ice make them particularly vulnerable to armed humans. The bears' natural curiosity, coupled with the attraction of carcasses being processed at sealing and whaling stations, exposed them to the danger of being shot everywhere people set up camp. All Arctic expeditions relied in large measure on polar bear meat for sustenance, and many bears were taken by whalers and other groups overwintering in the Arctic. It was mainly due to the ease of hunting polar bears that Vilhjalmur Stefanson, a famous nineteenth-century Arctic explorer, misled the public by describing the Arctic as a friendly environment. Although then, as now, the Arctic can hardly be described as friendly, he was correct in his assertion that the presence of polar bears made stocking the larder an easy task.

It was not only the newly arrived Europeans who were exploiting polar bears. A people known as the Pomors had settled the coasts of the White and Barents Seas in Russia as early as the eleventh century. By the fourteenth and fifteenth centuries, they had expanded their operations to the archipelago of Svalbard, and by the seventeenth and eighteenth centuries, the annual take of polar bears in Svalbard was over 200 bears. Harvests remained at approximately 200 bears a year until the end of the nineteenth century and the early twentieth century, when records show that Norwegian hunters were harvesting

The polar bear is one of the most difficult species on Earth to study. Even with highly sophisticated modern technology employed in polar bear research, we still have many gaps in our knowledge of the species and no reliable methods to monitor its population.

about 300 bears from Svalbard every year. On the Russian island of Novaya Zemlya, polar bear harvesting has had a similarly long history. In the western Russian Arctic, only Franz-Josef Land remained a refuge for the bears—at least until the end of the nineteenth century—due to its remoteness and harsh ice conditions.

American and Russian scientists work together on satellite-telemetry tracking of polar bears from the Chukchi-Alaskan population. Each bear is provided with a transmitter, and weighed and measured before released.

Polar bears were hunted for their pelts and for meat to feed local people and Arctic expeditions. According to available estimates, during the past 250 years 20 to 25 percent of the world harvest of polar bears has come from the Chukchi Sea in the eastern Arctic, and about 10 to 20 percent has come from the Kara, Laptev, and East Siberian Seas in the central Arctic. Polar bears from the western Barents Sea constitute the remaining 60 to 65 percent of the total polar bear harvest in Eurasia.

Before the beginning of the twentieth century, polar bears had already been eliminated from parts of their range. A unique population on St. Matthew Island in the northern Bering Sea, for instance, was extinct by 1900. Most of the St. Matthew polar bears used to pass the summer on the island when the sea ice receded north. Unfortunately, the island's location suited the needs of whalers and sealers as well. Difficulty getting to Wrangel Island protected polar bears there until 1921, when the first group of settlers attempted to establish a colony. Regular harvesting of bears, however, did not begin until 1926, when a permanent settlement was established on the island.

The heyday of polar bear extermination occurred in the 1950s and 1960s, when trophy hunting became fashionable and technological progress provided the means for people to move around in the High Arctic. About 70 percent of all polar bears killed in Alaska in the 1950s were shot from airplanes; in the 1960s this figure increased to 90 percent. In Norway, small ships brought sport hunters to shoot polar bears in the Barents Sea. During this twenty-year period, a total of 1,200 polar bears were killed

As this polar bear sleeps, human civilization and the rapidly increasing industrialization of the Arctic encroaches into its territory. Drilling, seismic testing, the construction of roads and pipelines, and other related industrial development are responsible for loss of habitat.

worldwide every year. Overall, since the beginning of the eighteenth century, it is estimated that at least 150,000 polar bears have been killed throughout the Arctic.

For all hunting methods except, perhaps, pursuit from aircraft, females with cubs were the most vulnerable segment of the population. On Wrangel Island, where polar bears were hunted mostly at dens, 80 percent of the bears killed were females with cubs. With the introduction of rifles to indigenous peoples, the balance between bear populations and traditional subsistence cultures broke down, and the hunters' take increased—influenced more by commercial interests than by subsistence requirements. It is thought that the unusual maternity denning of the Beaufort Sea polar bears out on the pack ice is due to the long persecution and extermination of breeding females on the Alaskan mainland.

The first hunting restrictions aimed at preventing the extermination of polar bears were instituted in the 1930s, when a decrease in polar bear numbers became apparent. In Russia, for example, in 1938, the administration of the Soviet North-East Passage State Department banned the shooting of polar bears from ships and at polar weather stations except in self-defense. In 1956, the hunting of polar bears in Russia (then, the Soviet Union) was banned completely. In Alaska, the first restrictions on polar bear hunting were implemented in 1948, although native people were allowed to harvest bears without limits until 1971, when the take was reduced by a quota system of three bears per hunter per year. In Norway, restrictions were introduced gradually beginning in 1957, when the government banned the capture of cubs and regulated hunting methods. Further steps taken in the 1960s finally led to the introduction of quotas for commercial and trophy hunting in 1970, and to a complete ban on bear killing in 1973.

An important step toward international cooperation in polar bear research and conservation was taken in 1965, when representatives from the five Arctic nations that span the range of the polar bear held a conference in Fairbanks, Alaska, at which they expressed the concern that overharvesting could push the species to extinction. Three years following this action, the International Union for the Conservation of Nature established a polar bear specialist group under the authority of the Species Survival Commission. The group meets every four years and is the leading authority on the polar bear's status worldwide. Eventually, further activities led to the signing of the International Polar Bear Treaty in 1973, which was ratified and put into effect in 1976. By signing the treaty, all Arctic nations assumed responsibility for protecting polar bears and their habitats, and for monitoring polar bear populations under their jurisdiction. Each nation implements the treaty according to its own national standards.

In Russia and Norway, polar bear hunting remains completely banned; only the killing of problem bears that threaten human lives or property is allowed by special permit. In the United States, the Marine Mammal Protection Act, passed in 1972, allows only native people to hunt polar bears—for traditional subsistence, clothing, and handicrafts—without restrictions on the number, sex, or age of bears. No commercial hunting is allowed in Greenland, but subsistence hunting by native residents is, with the requirement that hunters use only traditional methods such as dogsleds and kayaks. In Canada, natives can hunt polar bears, but the harvest is regulated by means of a quota distributed among villages, and there is a closed season to reduce the take of females with cubs. There is concern among conservationists, however, that Canada is in violation of the treaty because it allows the sale of shooting permits by native hunters to outsiders.

Polar bear females normally have litters once every three years. Native people of the Arctic prefer to hunt females with cubs because they consider the cub meat the most delicious.

Strict polar bear protection in the vast Eurasian section of the Arctic during the past decades, and the change from unlimited polar bear kills by native people in North America and Greenland to allowed quotas have been wildlife conservation successes. Polar bear numbers have grown, and most populations appear to be healthy. The polar bear, however, has not changed its basic nature nor has it moved from its harsh but vulnerable environment; it remains a fragile species with recent gains on shaky ground.

Unregulated or improperly regulated hunting is one of the two major threats for the polar bear. Currently, subsistence polar bear hunting in Alaska eliminates too many females, more than should be taken for the sustained use of the population. Alaskan polar bear biologist Dr. Steven Amstrup reported that during the last decade, for every sixty-one females eliminated (by all causes) from the Beaufort Sea population, only fifty-six are recruited. The polar bear is especially vulnerable to overharvesting because of its low reproduction rates and low population densities. Calculations based on long-term monitoring of polar bear populations in the Canadian Arctic indicate that if more than 1.5 percent of the adult females are eliminated annually, the population will decline.

The same habits that permit polar bears to survive on the ice make them particularly vulnerable to armed humans.

Generally, there is concern that so-called subsistence hunting is not properly managed. In Alaska, the sex has not been reported for 15 to 34 percent of all bears taken by native hunters since 1980, and there is evidence that most of the unreported kills were females. And there is more to this problem. What is called "subsistence" hunting is no longer a traditional hunt when motorized vehicles and modern rifles are used, or when native people sell their shooting rights to trophy hunters, as they do in the Canadian Northwest Territories.

The situation is no better in Russia. With the advent of economic and political reforms, polar bear protection has dropped dramatically throughout the Russian Arctic. The new market economy in Russia has created a demand for polar bear parts—skins and gall bladders—and food shortages in remote Arctic villages and polar weather stations have provoked the killing of bears for meat. Today poaching is the primary cause of polar bear mortality in Russia, and the extent of the loss is unknown. The majority of the poaching occurs along the north coast of Chukotka in Siberia and on the Taimyr Peninsula, where the ranges of polar bears overlap with human settlements.

The other serious threat to polar bears and their habitats is the rapidly increasing industrialization of the Arctic. Drilling, seismic testing, the construction of roads and pipelines, and other related industrial development may disturb polar bears directly, causing increasing losses of animals and habitat abandonment. These activities may also disturb bears indirectly. Oil and gas exploration and exploitation on the Arctic continental shelf may have catastrophic results if key polar bear breeding and hunting habitats are not strictly protected. There is no oil industry without oil spills, and if that happens in an Arctic marine area, there will be no way to deal with the consequences. An example of what we can expect with oil development on the Russian side was well illustrated in 1994 when, in violation of federal nature protection laws, all of Herald Island, which is part of a strict nature preserve, was included in the area planned for oil leasing. Fortunately, strident international protest by environmental groups was successful in halting the initiative.

Creating protected terrestrial and marine areas in the Arctic to conserve major polar bear breeding and hunting habitats is of prime importance to assure a secure future for the species. These measures, combined with proper management of subsistence harvests, law enforcement, and restrictions on industrial activities, are actions we know how to apply. However, there are other threats, threats of a global nature, such as pollution of the Arctic Ocean by toxins and radio-nucleids, and global warming, which we have only recently recognized and do not yet clearly understand. Even more uncertain is our ability to bring these threats under control. The first evidence that these factors are coming into play is troubling. In the Barents Sea, a large basin that accumulates contaminants from all over the Atlantic region and northeastern Europe, polar bears have been found to have extremely high levels of toxins in their bodies. As third- or fourth-level consumers, polar bears concentrate all the chemicals accumulated from the bottom of the food chain on up. These compounds may seriously affect reproduction and behavior, and we can only guess at what the repercussions will be in future generations of bears.

Whatever the factors currently affecting polar bear populations in different parts of the Arctic—hunting, oil exploration, shipping, pollution, or global warming—in combination their negative effects are magnified. The polar bear is at the top of the Arctic ecosystem, and whatever goes wrong at the lower levels of the system will be reflected in the polar bear's condition. The species is a natural indicator for monitoring Arctic marine ecosystems. The polar bear's health is also a yardstick against which we can measure our will—and our ability—to prevent the destruction of the Arctic.

Exterminated almost to extinction in the course of Arctic conquest by "civilized humans," then partly recovered during many years of strict protection, the polar bear remains a fragile species in our modern world. Its future is in our hands.

Polar Bear Facts

Species: *Ursus maritimus*

Common names: polar bear, sea bear, ice bear, white bear, nanook

Average weight: Male: 770 to 1,320 pounds (350–600 kg); a few over 1,760 pounds (800 kg); maximum recorded 2,201 pounds (1,002 kg)

Female: 330 to 880 pounds (150–400 kg), 50 to 75 percent less than males; maximum (on entering dens in autumn) 1,100 pounds (500 kg)

Average length (excluding tail): Male: 6.5 to 8 feet (200–250 cm); maximum recorded 10 feet (302 cm)

Female: 5 to 8 feet (160—250 cm)

Average height (at the shoulders): 52 to 56 inches (130–140 cm); rarely 60 inches (150 cm)

Longevity: 20 to 25 years; maximum 25 to 30 years

Color: Hairs are hollow and colorless. Actual color varies between white, yellow, gray, or even brown, depending on light conditions and lifestyle at the time.

Top speed: 24 miles per hour (40 kph)

Age at sexual maturity: Male: 3–5 years (in the wild males are able to compete for females when they are 6 years old). Female: 4–5 years

Frequency of reproduction: Every 3 years. The peak of reproductive ability in females is between 10 and 19 years of age.

Size of cubs at birth: Male: 12 inches (30 cm) Female: 11 inches (28 cm)

Range: Throughout the circumpolar Arctic. Northernmost record: 89° 30' N; southern extent of range: 50° in Canada; 79° in Svalbard (Norway)

Index

Recommended Reading

Matthews, Downs. Photographs by Dan Guravich. *Polar Bear.* San Francisco: Chronicle, 1993.

Ovsyanikov, Nikita. *Polar Bears: Living with the White Bear.* Stillwater, Minn.: Voyageur Press, 1996.

Stirling, Ian. Photographs by Dan Guravich. *Polar Bears.* Ann Arbor, Mich.: University of Michigan Press, 1988.

Walker, Tom. Photographs by Larry Aumiller. *The Way of the Grizzly.* Stillwater, Minn.: Voyageur Press, 1998.